With Love, a Human

Gloria Xiang

BookLeaf Publishing

Presentation by *BookLeaf Publishing*

Web: www.bookleafpub.com

E-mail: info@bookleafpub.com

ISBN: 978-93-5761-051-3

First edition 2022

PREFACE

accept yourself for who you are,
and love yourself for who you'll be.

Patient

i've never been the patient type.
ever since I've liked to read,
which is probably forever,
i have always opened a new book
to its last page before its first.
if only life were as simple as books;
then the creases of worry etched on my head
would only soften
as i await
my inevitable finale.

Warmth

2

is it possible to be in a constant state of warm,
soothing hugs?
i wish those days
would last as long as the days of stress.
perhaps I'll look back on these times
and remember
the small, happy moments
rather than the never-ending anxious ones.

Content

sometimes my heart feels like the moon
sometimes waned, sometimes filled.
my heart is the moon,
needing to change phases
just to feel whole again.
is it possible to always be content?
asks my heart,
as it continues to shrink and grow.

Hope

today, my fingers can't seem to hold on
but someday, i know they will.
today, i feel lost in the chaos of it all
and can't handle the weight of worry
but i still remember that someday, i will.
today, i feel like nothing can lift me off my
knees
but i know, that today, hope will.

Passion

unexpected discoveries
light me on fire.
i let the spark consume me,
and before i know it,
i am nothing more
than an ever-burning flame.

Love

love is immature.
innocent and childlike,
with no thought
of what tomorrow's troubles may bring.
and still, i will promise and whisper,
"forever."

Pain

two little pieces of me died
when my little pet birds passed away.
i was nine.
i remember praying to God
to send them back from heaven
and have their little wings carry them down.
i was naive then, and i am still naive now.
every time i hear the chirp of a bird
outside my window,
i find myself looking, hoping,
that God has answered my prayer.
pain is knowing that it will never happen.

Envy

over time, i have learned
that envy isn't always about clothes,
or looks, or money, or shoes.
sometimes i find myself
envying the way others
love themselves so dearly,
or don't cry, when i would most definitely cry
in the same situation.

Calm

calmness is release.
and so my soul sings
when i quiet my mind
and let every trouble
melt away like snow.

Homesick

to sleep on a mattress
in a new room
in a new house
in a new city
not knowing if the deep, longing knot
will go away
or if this foreign place
will ever feel like home.

Pride

there is a fine line
between self-assurance and pride.
i've made myself weak
just to avoid turning into
an ego-boosted monster.
a time will come when i realize the difference.
someday.

Bliss

i want to experience
opening up a storybook for the first time.
the anticipation and delight
of a brand new adventure
is my version of bliss.

Hate

the one thing that i hate
hate hate hate
more than anything
is impossibility.
if the universe is forever expanding
and if four babies are born every second
how is impossibility
even a possibility?
i hate that it creates lines that
i know i can never cross.

Alienated

how sad that this feeling
is so commonly shared
in the classrooms of children.
if i were God,
i would create a world with no borders,
with only love and acceptance.

Safe

books are my haven.
i have found that people are unreliable,
but books? Ink and paper
will never change.
its woven stories
hug me
and erase my worries.

Weary

somedays i feel as if
i am a single thread
holding on for dear life.
as if the thread will be blown away
with the slightest wind.

Nervous

i don't think it's possible
to ever be completely ready.
nervousness is a part of everyone,
so don't wait for a perfect time:
when you're just a little bit
more excited and confident
than nervous,
take the first bold step.

Fulfilled

i am here now.
Yesterday will not hurt me,
and Today will hold me in its arms
as i pursue nothing more
than just living
and laughing
and loving myself to the fullest.

www.ingramcontent.com/pod-product-compliance
Lightning Source LLC
LaVergne TN
LVHW051249200726
843510LV00011B/1754